CAT TALES

LESSONS IN LOVE FROM GUIDEPOSTS

DIMENSIONS
FOR LIVING

NASHVILLE

CAT TALES

98 99 00 01 02 — 10 9 8 7 6 5 4

This book is printed on acid-free recycled paper.

Library of Congress Cataloging-in-Publication Data

Cat tales: lessons in love from Guideposts.
     p.   cm.
   ISBN 0-687-01366-6 (paperback: acid-free recycled paper)
   1. Christian life.   2. Cats—Religious aspects—Christianity.
I. Guideposts (Pawling, N.Y.)
BV4501.2.C347   1994
242—dc20   94-33296
                                                                  CIP

Scripture quotations are from the King James Version of the Bible.

MANUFACTURED IN THE UNITED STATES OF AMERICA

All things bright and beautiful,
all creatures great and small,
All things wise and wonderful:
the Lord God made them all.

Cecil Frances Alexander, 1848

CONTENTS

FOREWORD

*W*hen God created animals, he must have made cats as a special gift. Let the rest of his creatures rove to prey on each other or add to the wonders and beauty of the world. Let some of them, such as cows and sheep, feed and clothe us; let others become beasts of burden. But cats he planned to be our companions, to live in our homes, to serve us in small ways, and mainly just to be loved and enjoyed as members of the family.

This book will make you want to tell your own cat stories. Although I already have one story in its pages, reading it now has unleashed another that goes back to my very first memories . . . of a cat named Dinah.

Dinah the cat chose to live in the barn. She was almost as big as my little sister, Gwen, who came lugging her up to the door one day. Standing on tiptoe, unable to reach the knob, she was crying out, "Open de door; I dot Dinah!"

This plea that struck us as so funny and sweet became a part of our vocabulary—one of those family jokes that nobody else would understand.

Over the years my sister and I have used it often by mail or phone to announce good news or bad. "Open de door; I dot Dinah!" meaning "Help, help! I need you; let me in!" or "Hooray! Listen— I've got wonderful news!" And whatever it means, we always laugh as we remember.

Such stories are so dear to a family. I urge you to write down yours, and ask your brothers, sisters, and parents too, if possible, to do the same. Then gather them into a little book that will preserve the memories for everyone. It will become a family treasure.

Meanwhile, here's a collection of cat tales from *Guideposts*. May you enjoy these mini "lessons in love."

Marjorie Holmes

MAKE UP YOUR MIND, OREO!

ARTHUR GORDON

*T*his morning our big cat, Oreo (so named because he is a handsome black-and-white), and I go through a familiar ritual at the back door.

Oreo has been outside for a while, and he really wants to come in. So I open the door and wait. But will he come in? No, he won't. He stops and lowers his head suspiciously, as if I were some deadly enemy. "Come on, Oreo," I say impatiently.

He sits down thoughtfully and begins to wash his face with one paw. Maddening.

"Oreo," I say, "I give you food. I supply all your needs. If you do anything in return, I don't know what it is. Now I'm personally inviting you into my house. So come on in!"

Oreo puts one foot across the threshold, then draws it back. He looks out across the yard with some remote, unfathomable expression. He still doesn't come in.

"Oreo," I say, "I'm not going to stand here forever. If you don't come in, I'm going to close this door. This is your last chance!"

I start to close the door slowly. Does he come in? No, he sits there, exercising his free will or something. He'll come when it suits him, not before. He figures I'll be patient. So far, he's right.

God made cats. He also made people. I wonder how he feels, sometimes, when he stands at the door and waits . . . and waits . . .

I think I know. 🐾

ON HIS OWN TERMS

MARJORIE HOLMES

*W*here Tiger came from we'll never know, nor where he goes when we're away. He simply sprang from the hedges one night when we drove in from our weekend at the lake, a striped gray tom, howling as if to demand, "Where have you *been?*" and entwining our legs like long-lost kin.

Because of our two dogs, we fed and bedded Tiger on the porch, thinking he'd surely be gone in a few days. But he promptly took up residence. And our instant, abiding love for him has never waned.

So it was with some regret that we left for a month's vacation that first year. Margaret, our next-door neighbor, agreed to feed him, but we doubted Tiger would be there when we returned. And sure enough it was true.

"Sorry about your cat," Margaret told us. "He hung around for a couple of days, then disappeared."

But as we stood mourning the inevitable, who should come scurrying up to purr his forgiveness and welcome but Tiger?

And thus it has been for almost four years. Mysteriously, he senses our homecoming. And no matter how long we may have stayed away, he comes rushing upon us, showing in every way he can how much he loves us, and how glad he is to have us home.

God is like that. No matter how far from him we stray, or how long we may be gone, he always faithfully awaits our return.

FOLLOWING THE VOICE

MARION BOND WEST

My husband, Gene, and I walked through our two pastures. We wanted the exercise, so we moved at a rapid pace. Our golden retriever, Elmo, ran ahead, excited. The grass was tall and the walking a bit rough. Several times I thought I heard a faint meow and we stopped, thinking there might be a stray kitten around. As we neared the end of our walk, something over a mile, I distinctly heard a loud meow. Gene, Elmo, and I stopped and listened. In the distance we saw a familiar figure jump up out of the tall grass, almost like a rabbit. It was our tiny bobtail kitten! She'd followed us all this distance, running to keep up. She must have frequently popped up out of the grass, which was well over a foot high, to determine our location.

"Oh, Bobbie," I cried, running back to her and lifting her to my shoulder. Usually a finicky kitten, she now nuzzled her head against me like a relieved child. I could feel her heart pounding. She licked my hands as I carried her back to the house, and she purred all the way.

Walking home, I thought, *I ought to be more like Bobbie.* Whatever my fear or need, from now on I will run straight toward the sound of God's voice, knowing that I am wanted and will be shown safely home.

"I WANT TO BE NEAR YOU"

CORA PETERS

*O*ur cat Lu-Lu recently had surgery. She is recuperating nicely but is still unable to jump around with her usual ease. This morning as I was having a cup of coffee and reading my devotional, she put her paws on my chair and attempted to leap onto my lap. She jumped part way and fell backward. To me, she seemed to be saying, "I want to be near you. Please help me up."

I tried to hoist her up, but she stiffened in pain. For some reason, I thought of how God works in my life. Sometimes I'm in pain, not so much physically but mentally as I agonize over some decision I have to make. I want God to be near, but my troubles make him seem far away.

Thinking of Lu-Lu again, I moved from my chair down onto the floor next to her. She moved easily into my lap. Lu-Lu curled up happily, contentedly, and went to sleep. Her reaction made me realize that I need not struggle to be near God; I can merely reach out to him, and he lovingly comes to embrace me with his presence.

UNTIL HEALING COMES

MARY E. MAUREN

*M*ourning was always a strange word to me—full of images of thick black veils, dirgelike music, and faces blank with forced-march resignation. When our twelve-year-old, Lawrence, died in a boating accident, our family was plunged into that world of mourning, and I was suddenly living out those images. I *felt* that thick black veil covering my bleeding heart. There was a dirge too—the unanswered questions, the pain-filled memories that kept the wound open. Though I had tried to walk hand-in-hand with God for many years, it was often agonizing effort and sometimes only pure decision that kept me going on my own forced march for my family's sake.

Perhaps the questions were the hardest part of that march. There was the day the whole family brought a garden gift to the cemetery. While my husband, Ray, and our other children searched for water for the plants, six-year-old Kris and I sat waiting by the graveside. I was holding tears in check, busily brushing grass clippings off the simple stone marker when I felt a tug on my coat.

"Momma, was Lawrence in that big box they put under the ground here?" I drew my son to me and rocked him in an embrace. Tears spilled over as I desperately looked to heaven for a wise way to explain, but nothing came to light.

"Where are you, God?" I cried inside. "Help me understand, or how can I ever help these little ones?"

That night I haltingly attempted an explanation as I snuggled Kris in bed. Three others crept in to listen and ask more hard questions. "I don't get it, Mom. When God saw the boat was in trouble, why didn't he do something?" "Why did God want Lawrence with him now?" "Am I going to die before I grow up?"

Memories, too, were so hard. There was the day that eleven-year-old Paul dug out Lawrence's trademark, his coonskin cap, to wear while riding his newly inherited bike. Seeing the flash of bike and hat going down the driveway opened the dike yet one more time. The same thing would happen when Lawrence's good friend Raelyn (who is also his sister) frequently played the tape from his last school concert. Pride and pain accompanied each flashback of Lawrence's first—and last—drum solo. Together our family avoided the silent drum set, his mitt and special blue aluminum bat and his penny collection. We had decided to set aside his "treasures" until we could decide when and how best to share them. Each question, each memory hurt so!

Weeks turned into months as I struggled through the alternatives of stoic resignation, emotional indulgence, and intellectual comprehension. They were all dead ends. Then, in a remarkable way, God showed me his simple truth.

The healing lesson began the day my son discovered our family cat on his bed, a swelling we had noticed on his forehead now an open wound. Together we got Tiger wrapped in a towel and to the vet, who diagnosed a deep abscess, probably resulting from a bite in a cat fight. The wound closed over on the outside, but kept festering underneath.

As the vet explained the seriousness of Tiger's condition and the need for antibiotic treatment and surgery, I stood washed again with the pain so easily triggered since the accident. Why this poor animal? Why this additional suffering?

Though my silent cries of "Why, God? Why more now?" were usually followed by "Thy will be done," it was said more with resignation than conviction.

That theme was repeated often through the next weeks as we tried to help Tiger recover. The vet gave instructions to open the wound daily and apply antibiotic powder each time until the healing progressed from the inside out. Each day was a painful trauma as someone had to catch the cat, wrap and hold him in a towel while another "operated."

After two weeks I called the vet to vent my utter frustration. "It's not getting any better. How can a wound heal if you open it every day?" The vet calmly reminded me that we were not just opening the wound, but were adding a healing antibiotic powder to it each time. He said there was no quicker way to heal an abscess that deep. We were to continue the procedure until we could see healing taking place inside to out. I hung up and cried, for I simply did not believe him.

It was another week before some slight improvement seemed to be taking place. And it was at this point I learned that one of my neighbors was moving. She was a woman who had continued to say "I am sorry your son is dead" by frequently sending over gifts from her garden and kitchen, though she had never called or come over herself.

I had not written any acknowledgment cards yet, so I thought I would walk across the street to thank Mrs. Burge before she moved. She met me at the door and invited me in with a sad smile. Tiny worry lines were etched over a face that somehow seemed much older than her fifty-odd years. We sat over tea as she apologized for never coming over after our tragedy, explaining how hard it was for her to face that particular kind of pain.

"You see," she said as she stared at the cup and saucer on her lap, "twenty years ago we lost . . . our only child when she was just . . . thirteen and . . ." A sob escaped her throat as she covered her face with her hands. I reached for her cup and set it on the table while struggling to free my own heart and voice. I searched for a way to respond that would not add to her hurt. For a few moments two broken-hearted mothers just sat wordlessly with each other. I did try to reach out to her with words of God's ultimate trustability, but I did not seem able to comfort her. I left with a heavy heart.

Taking the long way home, I pondered it all again. Wearily I asked God if *my* broken heart could ever be whole again. Then suddenly, dazzlingly, the whole situation of the cat's deep wound and slow recovery flashed before my mind. Surely, surely, that was it! For twenty years Mrs. Burge had had a festering wound—opened frequently, but evidently not filled each time with a healing substance that would have allowed healing from the inside out.

It was like the sun shining through after a hard rain, for now I knew I had a choice after all. Over the coming years the choice will not be whether to open the wound of Lawrence's tragic accident and death. That will often be beyond my power as other people or situations inevitably call forth the memory. Rather, the choice will be each time to invite and allow God's healing love to fill the open wound—submerging and washing the unanswered questions and raw edges of pain in the balm of his wisdom, his comfort, his healing wholeness.

Yes, the day came when we did not need to wrap the cat, open the wound, and apply the healing powder. Tiger's skin finally drew together in complete wholeness. I, too, am recognizing—almost two years after our tragedy—an inner pulling together into wholeness, a little more after each time of applying God's healing love. I am recognizing his special kind of healing taking place in me—from the inside out.

'FRAIDY CAT—JESSICA

MARION BOND WEST

*M*y five-year-old cat, Jessica, was terrified of the vacuum cleaner from the time she was a kitten. Often the vacuum and I would surprise her by entering a room where she was sleeping. Instantly her eyes would flash open, her ears flatten in fear, and she would dart out of the room in panic.

One day as I took out the vacuum, I spoke to her in my most gentle, reassuring voice: "It's all right, Jess. Trust me. You're okay. Stay put, kitty." The usual terror filled her eyes, and her ears flattened back, but she remained curled up on the bed as I vacuumed around it. This happened again . . . and then again. Finally the day came when she would open one sleepy eye, glance at the vacuum in ho-hum fashion, and continue her nap.

I learned something from Jessica. You can't outrun fear. Sometimes you just have to stand your ground. Jessica ran for five long years, but now she can claim victory over her mortal enemy, the vacuum cleaner. Like Jessica, I'm learning to heed that Voice that comes to reassure me when something frightening looms on the horizon of my life and I am tempted to flee in panic. Standing fast is difficult at times, but when the victory comes—as it surely will—what joy and peace we have won!

'FRAIDY CAT—MINNIE

MARION BOND WEST

*F*ear was creeping up on me as I sat in my livingroom. I needed to confront a neighbor who I felt had slighted me, and as I tried to pray about it, confusion mounted and my prayer felt empty. Suddenly, our new stray cat, Minnie, jumped on my lap. It took me a moment to realize that she was fearful. She stood almost paralyzed, staring at something with her ears flattened and her eyes widened.

Finally, I located the source of her fear. Minnie had seen my china cat sitting under a table. The statue looked quite lifelike. I picked it up to let my cat see that it wasn't real. She immediately buried her head under my arm and refused to look. I stroked her and talked to her, and gradually she lifted her head, still clinging to my arm. Ever so slowly Minnie sniffed the large china cat. Then she cautiously placed one of her paws on the statue's pink nose. She looked at me in astonishment and then with pleasure. She began to purr. I put the china cat back under the table, and Minnie hopped down and sauntered over to sniff it once more . . . maybe even to become friends.

Watching her walk confidently around the statue I thought, *Father, I do believe you can teach me about fear and trust, even from a cat!*

I went to the door. I would call on my neighbor and reach out past my fear. And with God's help, maybe even find the way to restored friendship.

THE PAPER CAT

FAY ANGUS

*M*y husband, John, and I are cat people. We rest best when lulled to sleep by the rhythmic *pur-r-r* of our marmalade cat, Ginger. She jumps to the foot of our bed, kneads the blankets, and nuzzles up to our feet before we turn out the light.

Imagine our shock the night that Ginger, who was not much more than a kitten, jumped onto the bed, suddenly arched her back, hissed and growled, sprang sideways, and rushed out of the room. In a few minutes she came slinking back, her eyes fixed on John. Quizzically we looked at each other, then followed her gaze to the large greeting card on his nightstand—our daughter's birthday selection for John. It was the head of a Siamese cat with enormous blue, luminous eyes!

"Ginger's terrified of a paper cat," I whispered to John. "Let's take it down!"

"No!" John whispered emphatically. "She needs to find out for herself that it's only paper and won't hurt her."

For half an hour we watched Ginger hiss and growl at the paper cat. Finally, she lunged at it with her paw, knocking it to the floor, where we left it for the night.

The next day we put the card back up. That night once again Ginger knocked it off the stand. It took several nights before she realized she had nothing to fear from the bright blue eyes of a *paper cat!*

Like Ginger's paper cat, so many of our fears are unfounded. For instance, I'd always been terrified of driving the tangle that is our California freeway system. "Come along, honey," my husband said to me recently. "It's really only another *paper cat!* You can do it." With this encouragement and with a lot of careful practice, I discovered I *could* drive the freeways without fear!

Now I quite enjoy freeway driving . . . as well as driving other unfounded fears away.

LETTING LOUIE KNOW

GLENN KITTLER

*W*hen I was a new cat owner, I read a newspaper article claiming that household pets, especially those that did not go outdoors, adjusted to the routines of their owners. Any sudden change of routine on the part of the owner could cause the animal to become upset or withdrawn. Working at home as I do, I thought that I spent plenty of time with my pet. But during some weeks my schedule was irregular and my cat would grow unusually quiet and distant. The article stated that when this kind of reaction occurred, the owner should explain the situation to the animal. Although the pet would not understand, at least it would not feel abandoned. I followed the article's advice—and it worked!

Late one afternoon I was preparing to leave my apartment with a visitor. I went over to my cat, who was perched on his favorite chair. "Now, Louie," I said, bending down to his level, "Mr. Davidson and I are going out for something to eat. You have everything you need, so you take care of the apartment and I'll be back around ten o'clock and I'll tell you all about it."

"What in the world are you doing?" my friend gasped. I told him about the newspaper article. He asked, "And that works?"

I nodded.

Halfway through dinner my friend said, "I've been thinking about you and your cat. Wouldn't it be nice if people communicated with one another like that? There would be less hurt, less argument, less pouting, less misunderstanding." I thoroughly agreed with him.

When I arrived home that night, Louie was waiting for me just inside the door. He arched his back and rubbed against my legs, purring all the while. I began to tell him about my evening. Yes indeed, my friend was right. Would that we humans could learn the art of communicating with one another. Love and understanding would surely follow. 🐾

LOUIE, THE TOUCHER

GLENN KITTLER

*R*ecently I attended a large cultural gathering of mostly strangers. I saw people greeting one another with smiles and handshakes, hugs and kisses, and an occasional touch to an arm or a pat on the back.

I probably wouldn't have given it a thought except that I heard a woman nearby say, "Have you noticed how people are always touching each other?"

The woman with her said, "Yes, I have. Why do you ask?"

"I don't like it," the first woman said. "Somehow it just seems like an empty gesture. It's meaningless."

Then I thought of Louie. People unfamiliar with the ways of cats may not believe this, but my cat Louie is a real toucher. He was about a month old when he moved in with me. Once he discovered where at home I work and spend most of my day, he decided to join me, curling up under the desk and resting his head on my foot. When I get up and move about, Louie follows me, and when

I go back to my desk, he curls up again and puts his head back on top of my foot.

This has been going on now for ten years. No matter where I happen to be in the apartment, Louie is there, too, touching me with a paw or brushing against me. I don't know whether he does this to let me know he is there or to be sure I am there, but I do know that I like it. And it gently tells me I'm wanted and needed.

No, a touch isn't an empty or meaningless gesture, it's a silent way of letting the heart say what really doesn't need to be said.

AND THEN, ALONG CAME TOBY

LOIS ALLEN SKAGGS

*W*e had a problem at our house that seemed almost hopeless. Cleo, my husband, had suffered two severe heart attacks and now, unable to work, he had taken to drinking. It was a familiar cycle: a period of sobriety, then a drinking bout, followed by remorse and another stretch of sobriety. Sometimes in those drying-out periods, I'd find him sitting on the edge of our bed, staring at the floor. The humiliation in his face—his sad brown eyes—would speak for him. "I hate myself. Just look what I'm doing to myself. I should be taking care of you."

Many times I'd think I couldn't go through it again. I'd cry out to God, "Oh, help this man who is so unhappy with himself. Help me; I don't know what to do. Please, please, take over."

And then, along came Toby. A kitten. My daughter Ann was in the process of moving to her own apartment, and Toby started out as her pet. "Mom," she said one day, "I bought a little Siamese cat. Can I bring him here till I move? Just for a few weeks?"

Inwardly I groaned. To me, pet spelled p-e-s-t. But what could I say? Ann had already bought him. "Okay," I said reluctantly. "But only till you move."

"Thanks, Mom." She grinned. "Oh, you'll love him; wait and see."

"I doubt that."

But, as I discovered, Toby was hard to dislike. He had limpid blue eyes—even tiny eyelashes. His fawn-colored coat was soft and shiny—long for a Siamese; his ears, paws, and "mask" a deep dark chocolate brown. He was the washingest kitty I'd ever seen. Lying in the sun on our back porch, he'd lick one little brown paw with his tongue and scrub his ear again and again, then do the other one.

I'd always heard that Siamese were likely to be aloof. Not this one. He actually seemed to cultivate us and seek affection. Especially from Cleo.

Shortly before her moving day, Ann got some bad news. "I can't take Toby with me, Mom. The landlord says 'no pets.' I guess I'll see if my friend Tammy can take him to her family's farm."

Cleo and I talked it over. When Ann moved, Toby stayed.

We let him come and go as he wanted. Soon I could open the back screen door, yell "Toby!" and he'd come running as fast as he could fly, his paws barely touching the ground. He ran after birds, butterflies. On his first excursion up our walnut tree, he got stuck. When it began to rain, we had to ask our neighbor Ron, who owns a tall ladder, to rescue him.

Before long, Toby established routines with Cleo and me. In the morning, he'd hop up on our bed, settle down between us, and purr us awake. When I came home from my job as a switchboard operator on the evening shift at Farmington Community Hospital, Toby met me at the back door—as if to remind me that he'd been doing *his* job of keeping Cleo company while I was gone. It was a job he took very seriously.

He played with Cleo constantly, and when Cleo took a nap, Toby curled up at the foot of the bed to take a nap, too. If Cleo watched television, Toby climbed into his lap. He followed Cleo everywhere. When Cleo worked in the yard, Toby had to inspect everything that was done. Cleo even asked his opinion.

"How's that, boy? Think that will do?"

Silence.

"Yeah, I think so, too."

When Cleo walked across the driveway to sit with Ron on his porch steps for a neighborly chat, Toby would follow and lie between his feet, patiently waiting. After the visit, Cleo would say,

"Well, Toby, let's be on our way," and off they'd go, Toby trailing behind.

Watching, smiling to myself, I'd think, *I do believe that cat thinks he's a dog.*

One evening Cleo was sitting in his favorite chair, a recliner, leaning back with his hands clasped behind his head. Toby jumped onto the table by the chair and meowed, looking intently at Cleo.

"What do you want, Toby?" Cleo said.

"Meow."

"What do you want, boy?"

"*Meow, meow,*" Toby cried, louder. Taking his hands down, Cleo leaned forward. "Toby, I don't know what you want!"

Toby promptly sprang up and stretched out full length along the top of the backrest. That was *his* favorite spot on Cleo's favorite chair.

When he told me about it later, Cleo said, "That boy can talk. He was telling me to move my arms out of the way."

Toby was telling Cleo something else, too. Something we didn't recognize till later.

After breakfast one morning, Toby went to the back door, meowed, and sat down. That meant he wanted out. Cleo opened the door, but Toby just sat still and looked up at him.

"Well, go on out, if you want, boy." Cleo nudged him lightly, so out he went.

An hour or so later, someone knocked at the front door. Cleo went to answer. I heard a man's voice. "Do you own a Siamese cat?"

"Yes, we do," Cleo replied.

"You'd better come with me," the man said.

I dropped to my knees. "Oh, no, Lord. Please, no!"

Cleo came in through the back door, his chin trembling so he could hardly get the words out. "Toby's been hit! Honey, he's dead."

"Oh, Cleo!"

"He's lying on the back porch. The man said he just couldn't help it. Toby jumped in front of the truck. He wasn't mangled; he looks like he's sleeping."

Cleo choked out the next words. "He loved me!"

"I know, honey."

"He loved me just the way I am."

"I know."

For a while, we didn't speak. Then I put my arms around him. "You know, Cleo, that's the way God loves you, too. Just like you are. His love is just like Toby's, only more. His love follows you, too."

We stood silently, holding each other, for a minute. Then Cleo went down to the basement and found an old tin breadbox and some soft cloth to line it with. He took it out to the back porch. I stayed inside. I didn't want to see Toby. I wanted to remember him alive.

From the window, I watched Cleo carry the box and a shovel down to the back of the garden where he and Toby had spent so much time together. He dug a tiny grave under the peach tree.

I bowed my head. "Lord, is it wrong to love a cat that much?"

The answer came gently, firmly, into my mind: *Through that cat, your husband has been able to feel my love. I sent Toby.*

"Oh, yes, Lord. Thank you."

I peeped out the window again. Cleo was just sitting on the ground, holding the shovel, his head bowed. He sat there a long time, telling Toby good-bye. From that time on the binges stopped. Cleo began going to church with me. No more than a month later—just before Christmas—he committed his life to Christ. As for me, I'm still learning every day that God's ways are "past finding out." He loves us so generously. So forgivingly. He can even use a little cat to show us that.

LOVE CAN WORK MIRACLES

BETTY R. GRAHAM

O ne Friday morning a few months ago, I had just walked into my office when the phone rang. I reached for it and heard my son's panicky voice: "Mom, you've gotta come home quick— Bootsie's been hit by a car!" I drove back home promptly, worrying about Brian. His cat meant a lot to him.

We rushed Bootsie to the Mount Vernon Animal Hospital and waited anxiously while the veterinarian's expert fingers gently probed the animal's limp body. Then she ordered X-rays. I knew the prognosis was bad when she called me aside in the hall. "I'm afraid that he doesn't have much of a chance," she whispered.

I swallowed hard. "Well, do what is necessary, Doctor. Don't let him suffer." I didn't know how I was going to tell my son.

When we entered the examining room again, Brian turned his tear-stained face to the doctor. "He *will* get better, won't he?" I could see how my fourteen-year-old son was struggling with his emotions and trying to act like a man. But the fear in his eyes belied his attempt at optimism.

"We'll do all we can, son," Dr. Prescott answered. "I'll have to keep him here awhile."

"We can come to see him, can't we?" Brian asked eagerly.

I'd never heard of visiting hours for cats, but the vet nodded. Did that mean that she wasn't going to put Bootsie out of his misery? I didn't ask.

In the car I tried to prepare Brian for the inevitable. We didn't seem to have much luck with pets. In the four years we had lived in Mount Vernon, Virginia, we had lost our little ten-year-old Yorkshire terrier, Timmy, and three other cats. Brian would get over the loss of one-year-old Bootsie, I told myself. After all, it was only a cat, and not a very affectionate one at that. He would all but knock me down to get at his food bowl, but once his fat tummy was filled he seemed to ignore me. I could stand on the front porch and call him again and again, and he would turn his back and go the other way.

"We'll get another cat right away," I said to Brian.

"But I don't want another one, Mom," he sobbed, giving in to the worry inside him. "I want Bootsie. He's my cat."

Like every mother, I have times in my life when I wish I had the power to grant the impossible dreams of my children, even though I know that disappointments help youngsters build the character and maturity needed to face adult life. I find it harder to deal with my boys' pain than with my own. At that moment, I would have given anything for a magic wand to wave over Bootsie. I wanted to be able to say, "Mommy fixed it, honey," as I had so often when Brian was growing up.

We drove to school, and I explained to the principal why Brian was late, asking that the teachers be a little understanding that day if he didn't concentrate fully on his studies. Then I returned to my office and dug into normal duties.

When I got home that afternoon, Brian met me at the door. "Can we go see Bootsie now?" he begged.

"Not today, Brian," I answered. "Dr. Prescott said we should wait until after the weekend." I changed the subject and started to prepare dinner.

I fixed Brian's favorite rice, and we played a game together after supper, but it was earlier than usual when Brian kissed me good-night. "Bootsie's got to be okay," he said. My heart ached for the child.

I went to bed, too. Lying there, trying to sleep, I heard sounds in Brian's bedroom. Thinking that he was crying again, I quietly went to comfort him. Moonlight shone through the windows of his room and, peeping in, I could see Brian's dark silhouette. He was on his knees beside the bed, his hands folded, whispering a prayer. " . . . and he never did anything bad to anybody. Please, God, *I know you can do it.*"

Aside from our daily grace at the table, I had not heard Brian speak aloud to God since the bedtime prayers we said together when he was small. When he reached his teens, his faith became private.

I tiptoed back into my room, feeling ashamed. Not once that day had I suggested that God might help. I call myself Christian and try to set an example for my children, yet I had not even thought of praying for a cat. But Brian had.

And why shouldn't he? Didn't God create all life, and isn't it precious in his sight? If it were not so, why would he direct Noah to save the animals?

I had looked at the odds and had given up immediately. But inside the heart of my loving son there was a spark of hope—and the childlike wisdom to know where to go for help. I knelt quietly beside my own bed and joined Brian in his petition.

On Monday morning I called Dr. Prescott. The veterinarian said that it wouldn't hurt if Brian came to visit his cat. "Bootsie's still alive," she told me, "but he won't eat. His chances are even slimmer if he doesn't take some nourishment. He won't have enough strength to get well."

Had the cat, too, given up?

That afternoon we went to the kennel area of the pet hospital. Dogs barked and cats meowed as we passed the metal cages. We found Bootsie stretched on his side, his eyes dull and glazed, his breathing labored. A portion of fur had been clipped from one hip, where the car had struck him. The cat's broken pelvis and ribs would heal, the vet told us, but other internal injuries caused more serious problems.

"Hey, Bootsie," Brian called softly. "How're ya doin', baby?" He gently stroked the sleek head, and the cat's tail twitched slighly. "You're gonna get better, Boots. I know you are!" Brian said confidently. "We love you."

The cat could not lift his head, though he opened and closed his eyes occasionally during the ten or fifteen minutes Brian stroked him and talked to him.

When we returned the next afternoon, Bootsie raised his head as Brian approached the cage, but his food remained untouched. Brian held the water bowl to Bootsie's lips, and the cat lapped a few times. Then Brian picked up the food bowl and offered a few crumbs on his fingers. The cat licked them off. A soft buzzing sound, an erratic purr, came from his throat.

The following afternoon, Boots was curled in his normal ball when we opened the cage door.

His green eyes, now clear and shining, looked up at my son with nothing less than adoration. The cat had eaten some of the food in his bowl, and with Brian's help he finished his meal. My son's joy reached new bounds when Boots struggled to stand so that he could rub his cheek against Brian's hand.

Four more days went by before we were allowed to bring Bootsie home. He limped badly, and I thought he would be crippled for the remainder of his nine lives. But today you'd never guess that the cat had been hurt. He's once again fat and sleek. He runs as fast and jumps as high as he ever did. The only difference I see in that cat is his undisguised devotion to my son. When Brian comes home, Bootsie runs over, stands up on his now-strong hind legs, and greets Brian with a "kiss."

My neighbor Pam expressed my own feeling on the day we brought Bootsie home from the hospital. "It was love that saved that cat," she said. "Love can work miracles."

Yes, it was love—the pure love of a young boy with faith, who cared enough to communicate his feelings to his pet. But more, it was the perfect love of God, who hears every sincere prayer.

I had wished for a flimsy magic wand. My son reached out for the greatest power in the universe—the power of God's love for us all.

TAFFY DOESN'T ASK FOR MUCH

SAM JUSTICE

*T*affy, our twelve-year-old cat, doesn't ask for much—a bed box in a heated garage, food in his bowl, a pan of water, and a little fellowship. I never have to walk him, comb his coat, or give him baths. Nature has well endowed him to care of these chores himself. It's just bed, board, and a bit of togetherness.

Taffy can sleep almost anywhere—spread out on the side porch or under a shady bush in mild weather, or, when it's chilly, curled up on top of a garaged car or in his box. It doesn't matter whether his food is wet or dry as long as it's steady.

What really turns him on, though, is being permitted to curl up on a seat in the dinette. He's not allowed into the rest of the house because of his obnoxious habit of clawing at rugs and the backs of upholstered chairs.

The crowning point of Taffy's day is to leap up onto a dinette chair, settle down, and snooze peacefully. And it's even better when there's somebody around to join him. The moment anyone sits down next to him, Taffy begins to purr like a motorboat. He's just happy to be a part of the scene, and as long as he has company, everything's purr-fect.

Taffy has helped me to realize how important it is for all of us to have friendly souls around us. It tells us they're glad we're here, glad to be near us, enjoy our company. In other words, we are appreciated. Now I can't purr like Taffy, but I can always say, "Glad you joined me. Nice to have you."

A SPECIAL KITTEN

MARGARET E. SANGSTER

*J*t was a cold, blustering night, and when I opened the door, in stepped the major, his coat dusted with snow. He kissed me and said, "I'm leaving right away, Aunt Margaret—have to be back at West Point by dawn."

"Can't I even give you a bite to eat?" I began, but he shook his head.

"No can do," he told me, "but there's something else you can do." He hesitated. "When I went past the library this morning, he was sitting in the deep snow. And when I started home for lunch, he was still sitting in the snow, so I picked him up. But we can't keep him at our house because of Butch." Butch was half Airedale and half coyote. "He isn't pretty, Aunt Margaret, but he has personality-plus!" He reached into his pocket and produced the very thinnest black-and-white kitten I'd ever seen. "You'll love him before the week's out!"

"You know I have two Persians and an Afghan already," I protested weakly, but the major's hand was resting on the doorknob.

"Your Persians will welcome a kitten," he said. "And the Afghan's used to cats. Be seeing you, Aunt Margaret!" He quickly left, and I stood with the trembling black-and-white kitten in my hands.

"What am I going to do with you?" I asked aloud. "I don't need you—I don't want you. You're homely!"

But before the week was out, the major's prophecy had come true. I *did* love the black-and-white kitten—maybe because he needed me. I named him Major, of course, for his West Point godfather.

I learned immediately that Major was indeed a personality kitten. In a matter of split seconds he made friends with my Persians and the Afghan hound, and he peered at me with an adoration I didn't deserve. He was unusual in other ways too.

One icy day a half-frozen bird fell into the largest drift in my garden, and Major lifted it in his mouth, gently, and carried it to me—he remembered what it was like to be half-frozen. He stood beside me, purring, as I fed the bird from a medicine dropper, and soon the bird recovered and went on its way rejoicing.

Major became the protector of all small wildlife in the area. I can't tell you how many chipmunks and squirrels he rescued from certain death at the paws of my Persians.

Time went on. We moved from a large house to a small one, then to an ancient farmhouse in the Berkshire Hills. But Major didn't object to a change of scene—home to him was any place in which I lived. I noticed, however, that he seemed to tire easily—he'd got off to a bad start physically.

One afternoon I went to the village market and as I came back into the house and dropped my bag of groceries on a stand in the hall, Major didn't come trotting to meet me as he usually did. I found him sleeping quietly in his favorite chair—too quietly. As tears ran down my cheeks, I knew something precious had gone out of my life.

How can I explain what this cat meant to me? Maybe, in some sense, I was allowed to be God's agent with this small life to teach me something. Major looked to me for comfort and love and assurance—as I have learned to look to God.

As I glance back across the years, I realize that at times I fell short of Major's faith and abused his trust. There was a blazing day in mid-summer when his water dish remained empty. There was a long night when he was unwittingly imprisoned in a storage closet. But I am sure his devotion for me never changed, despite my carelessness.

Major was only a cat—and a cat's life is both short and trivial in a world where so many humans know hunger and grief. But even so, that life contributed happiness. And so I am wondering if it might be possible for the Almighty to find a small place for him in heaven. Perhaps there is some unclaimed corner, cozy and forgotten, where a kitten can purr a rhythmic response to the angels' song.

JASPER, YODA, AND JESUS

MARGIE NADINE WALKER

I silently prayed for wisdom as I watched my twelve-year-old daughter, Kris, print these words on a large cardboard sign: LOST— BLACK KITTEN—NAMED "YODA"—$10 RE- WARD. For the past four days after school, we had canvassed the neighborhood door to door, posted signs, and placed a "lost kitten" ad in the paper. Then, hoping to catch a glimpse of him, we walked and drove up and down the surrounding streets. But Yoda had disappeared.

From the very beginning, as soon as we discov- ered he was gone, we had prayed for Yoda. Now, as our little girl began to realize that we probably would never see him again, I yearned to find reassuring words to tell her. "Please, God," I prayed, "don't let her faith in you be shattered because of this. What can I say to her if we can't find her kitten?"

Our family's adventure with cats had started two years earlier, when *we*—yes, *we*—were adopted by a large, older, striped-gray cat, whom we named Jasper. He was "king" of the backyard, very dignified, and for the past two years had reigned supreme over the neighborhood. Appearing to be hostile and gruff, he was really putty in our hands, gentle and loving.

One day I jokingly pointed out to my husband that what Jasper needed was a little kitten to play with (preferably black, because Kris and I loved black cats—they're so sleek and shiny . . . and special!). And guess what? I had just found one in a "free kitten" ad. Larry, who was not a cat lover, shook his head. "Jasper'll never accept another cat," he said. "I think you're just asking for trouble." But he didn't object, so Kris and I answered the ad and went to pick him up.

The kitten was hiding in a corner of the garage in a laundry basket. He was solid black, with a tiny nick on his chin. Kris loved him instantly. We took him home and named him "Yoda," for an outer-space character in the *Star Wars* movie series.

In the first days, Yoda settled into our family with no effort at all. He was an adventurous kitten who liked to ride in our car with us and loved to ride in the basket of Kris's bicycle.

But Jasper did not take easily to the newcomer. He seemed insulted to have his domain threatened and was prone to ignore Yoda, only looking up to hiss as Yoda slid into feeding time like a baseball player stealing second. Undaunted,

Yoda treated Jasper like his dearly loved older brother, always running expectantly toward him and trying to play with him. Yoda's day was complete when he could snuggle up beside Jasper on the crocheted afghan, kneading it with his paws and purring himself to sleep. Never mind that Jasper, ever superior, totally ignored him.

It was about this time that Kris, who was always quick to express herself through art, started drawing cartoons about the two cats. Kris believed that when we weren't watching them, Jasper played with Yoda, giving him advice, taking pleasure in his company. And so Kris's drawings showed a kindly older cat telling the "new cat on the block" important things about life on Earth, things like God's love and the need to pray and sing praises. There were cartoons of Jasper wearing a cape and flying through the sky on secret missions, with Yoda on his back, showing him the wonders of God's creation. From that time on we dubbed him "Bat Cat."

In the second week or so, I began to think that maybe Kris had the right idea: I'd see Jasper watching Yoda intently, his ears pitched forward. Occasionally I even saw him batting Yoda playfully with his paws, and once I caught him bathing Yoda's face—but *never* when Jasper thought I was watching.

This was the state of affairs when, about six weeks later, Yoda, not wearing his identifying collar, wandered away, probably chasing a butterfly. Kris and I were heartbroken.

And so the search began. With each fruitless day that passed, we continued to hope and make plans for the next day. "Tomorrow we'll try this . . . or that," we said. But soon we had looked everywhere with no sign of the lost kitten. I put my arm around Kris as she buried her face in my shoulder, not wanting me to see her tears. "Mom, if I could just know that someone was taking care of him," she said. "Or if he had to die, at least know he didn't suffer. I could even accept it if he found a good home, with someone who loved cats the way we do. But I just keep picturing him out there . . . all alone . . . and it hurts so bad."

I knew exactly how she felt and realized then that I was worried not only about Yoda but about Kris as well. *I need help, Lord,* I prayed silently. *Just give me wisdom. I can't carry this alone anymore, so I'm giving it all to you. Please help me trust you and find words now that will help Kris.*

Turning to her, I began, "Kris, we *must* give this problem to Jesus. He cares, and he really is the only One who knows the total situation. Can you believe—*even* if you never see Yoda again—that he just went for a walk with Jesus? Can you trust that Jesus will take care of him?"

We prayed together then. Just a simple prayer, asking Jesus to take care of Yoda. And I hugged Kris. I really didn't expect what happened next. Kris's face lit up for the first time in days, and she raced from the room. Cartoons began flying off her notebook paper again, as she grasped the concept of a little cat "going for a walk with Jesus."

There were pictures of Jesus and Yoda—riding a bike together, frolicking through heaven (to the dismay of several angels), exhaustedly taking a nap on the clouds and then sitting at the table eating together.

So clearly did these drawings reflect her happiness—and faith—that as she shared them with me, we began to laugh, and then cry at the same time. It was with complete trust that Kris said, "Mom, it's okay. I know that if I never see Yoda again, Jesus will take care of him."

Yes, I thought, *it is okay*. Only God could have chosen such a unique way of answering my prayer. What a beautiful reminder that, no matter what my own problems, God will always have a custom-designed, just-for-me answer.

Then, ten days after Yoda disappeared, a telephone call came from Mary Simms, a "cat-loving" woman who had just read our ad in the weekly paper. We rushed over to find Yoda happily playing on the patio with her cats—on what looked like a feline gymnasium.

Together we learned that, to get to her house, Yoda had crossed three very busy main streets, had traveled one and a half miles (in a direction we hadn't even looked), and had narrowly missed being hit by several cars as his rescuer watched helplessly from her kitchen window.

Many times Mary had attempted to coax him from his hiding place with food, but having been chased into thick ivy by dogs, Yoda was terrified. Finally she was able to rescue the starving kitten and take him home with her.

A peek into our home that evening, after we brought Yoda back, would have revealed quite a scene. As Yoda was put down on the floor, a look of wonderment crossed his face. He looked around and sniffed the air for a few minutes. Suddenly he ran toward the kitchen and slid into the feeding dish like a baseball player stealing second. Yes, Jasper was there, but this time he licked Yoda's face as if to say, "Welcome home."

Later we put the two cats in the garage, where they always slept at night in baskets on top of the chest freezer. Next morning, on his way to the car, Larry let the cats into the house. As Kris and I bent to kiss them, we were met with the lingering odor of after-shave lotion wafting from their foreheads! We just looked at each other and smiled.

COME BOLDLY

MARION BOND WEST

*M*y husband, Gene, and I know what to expect a few moments after we go to bed and turn off the light. It has become a nightly routine. Minnie, who isn't a very courageous cat, will pad softly into our room, hesitate for a few moments, then spring gently onto our bed. She settles down in between our feet. I suppose because it's dark and still, she thinks we don't know she's there. But usually one of us says, "Hello, Minnie. We know it's you. You're welcome to come and sleep with us. You don't have to sneak in after the light is off."

Still, she comes only when it's dark and our voices have quieted. *Poor Minnie. She needs to become more . . . bold,* I thought, just before I drifted off to sleep. Then my eyes popped open. Another thought came quietly, but defiantly. *I would like for you to come to me, child, without such hesitancy, also. Sometimes you come almost apologetically, wondering if you'll be received. Come to me, boldly.*

Right then and there, I approached my Father with a problem I had thought too small to bring to him. In my mind, I sat in his lap like a small child and explained, "It's income tax time again, Father. I've procrastinated long enough. In the morning, will you help me to organize what I must do?"

And then I turned over and went to sleep. I liked the sound of Minnie purring at the foot of our bed.

MEANT FOR EACH OTHER

ANN KINDIG

I'd thought my life was complete: marriage, two healthy sons, a house filled with books. And then, when our sons were in college, my thirty-year marriage ended in divorce and left me feeling totally rejected and unlovable.

My face in the mirror became a gloomy reminder of what I'd lost. Family and friends were supportive, but I felt a huge void in my life. I prayed to feel whole again.

One day a friend telephoned to tell me that an elderly neighbor had gone to a nursing home and had to leave his Manx cat behind. "I thought of you immediately," my friend said. But I wasn't interested in taking on a cat. Later the phone rang again: "I know of a cat who needs a home," another friend said. "A Manx . . ."

A Manx? The kind that doesn't have a tail? Why should I want a cat without a tail? I politely declined.

To keep busy I attended divorce recovery workshops, shopped with friends who told me to change my image, sat through seminars, and read self-help books by the dozen. The face in my mirror reflected newly improved makeup but little joy.

Then yet another friend called. "Have I told you about this cat named Twink?" she said. "She's a Manx who—"

All right, all right, if people were so determined to give me a Manx, maybe I should see one. A meeting was arranged, and I was less than awed. Twink was black as midnight, fat and dumpy. Her back legs were so long they made her seem to lumber, and when she walked, her stomach swayed from side to side. And she wasn't really tailless—she had a little corkscrew of a stub.

Twink, I learned, had been abandoned at a resort and taken to a shelter, where workers couldn't bear to destroy her. Then along came the elderly gentleman who took her in. When he left his home, Twink was alone again, and that's where my friends came into the picture. And the amazing thing I discovered was that not one of the three friends who called me knew that the others were suggesting that Twink and I were meant for each other.

"Okay, I'll take her," I said finally. It seemed to me that God wanted me to have this cat.

Twink came into my home, sniffed around, then methodically rubbed her scent on everything from the furniture to the flowerpots. Then she defended her territory in a noisy nose-to-nose-through-the-glass confrontation with Gertrude, the huge orange cat from next door. But it wasn't until I awoke at night and found her pressed against my side that I comprehended that *I* was the one who had been adopted.

Now I grew curious about this special kind of cat, and I was particularly pleased with a story someone told me about Twink's lack of tail. "When the Manx cat hurried to board Noah's Ark," a friend explained, "Noah accidentally shut the door on its tail!"

I hadn't anticipated that my homelife would turn into a slapstick routine, with Twink galloping to greet me at the door. It was difficult to stay depressed when Twink sprawled like an ape to groom herself, tumbled over like a beanbag when she wanted her stomach scratched, and made Tarzan-like noises as she bounded onto my bed. At night Twink snuggled in my lap while I read, her stubby nontail twitching in time with her contented purr.

And gradually as I laughed at Twink, I began to laugh in the rest of my life. I took on some new duties at work and helped organize some projects that excited me at church. Life was good again.

Then came the morning that Twink and I watched as Gertrude, the neighbor cat, sauntered across our outside deck. As Twink crouched at the patio door with hackles raised, Gertrude decided to show off. Turning and twisting with the grace of a matador, she swished her fluffy tail like a cape. Twink was infuriated, but I was amused. "Don't pay any attention to her, Twink," I said. "That long tail serves no purpose at all. Who needs it anyway?"

Who needs it anyway? Slowly I saw the connection. A part of my life was gone now; at one time it had been a wonderful part. But just as Twink could carry on without a tail, I could have a happy life without a marriage.

Twink was whole, and her lack of a tail made her no less so. And now I knew why the face in my mirror had been smiling so much lately: I was whole too. The answer to my prayer had come in the form of a cat who walked like an Angus steer, ate like a pig, and lounged around like an orangutan.

Once I'd thought my life was complete. Well, it was *still* complete. Noah might have shut the door on the Manx's tail—but God hadn't shut his door on either one of us. 🐾

THE CAT IN THE CONSPIRACY

ALETHA LINDSTROM

*O*nly *eight o'clock and already this house is like an oven,* I thought irritably. Setting my coffee cup on the kitchen counter, I reached across the sink to close the shutters against the intense July heat. Just before they clicked shut, I glimpsed some small animal moving along a fencerow in the far pasture. A cat.

Another animal dumped, I decided—and felt a rush of anger at callous pet owners who abandon unwanted cats and dogs along country roads. But the incident was soon forgotten, swallowed by a deeper anger that had been seething inside me since an argument with my husband, Andy, the night before.

It was one of those times when he took charge of decision-making in a way that made me feel my own opinion and role in the matter were belittled—or so it seemed to me. I'd responded sarcastically in a way well calculated to wound his pride. He'd made an angry reply. And so it built until we thoroughly disliked each other.

By bedtime we weren't speaking, and the silence continued through breakfast. I remembered the set look on his face as he shoved his chair away from the table, grabbed his briefcase, and stalked silently out the door. Not one word of apology. Not even a *good-bye*.

This hadn't happened before in our twenty years of marriage. Like all husbands and wives, we exchanged occasional sharp words. But never had our anger lasted this long. And never had I felt so humiliated, so rejected. I refused to consider that Andy's usual good humor had been sabotaged by hot, sleepless nights—and by eight hours of daily sweltering in an office without air-conditioning. I refused to consider that I, too, was extremely edgy from a week of record-breaking temperatures.

Instead I nursed my grievance. "He'll probably come home expecting all to be forgiven and forgotten," I muttered. My bitter mood intensified as I cleared away coffee cups, untouched toast, and bowls of half-eaten cereal. I lifted Andy's chair to replace it by the table. Suddenly I felt an urge to retaliate. "Well, it *won't* be forgotten! I'm tired of being treated like a child!" I slammed the chair down. "Maybe I won't even be here!" I said. "Let him find out how it feels to be walked out on!"

The boldness of the idea frightened me. Yet I felt determined—and strangely exhilarated. But where could I go? To relatives? To a motel? I'd have to think about it. Then some inner voice warned: *Get out of the house. Take a walk. Consider this carefully before you do something you'll regret!* I glanced at the clock. Eight-thirty. I still had plenty of time.

My energy, fueled by my need to get even, propelled me rapidly down the country road. The sun burned through my thin blouse, but I was more aware of the resentment simmering inside me. As I walked along, kicking angrily at stones, I dredged up old hurts and insults, building my case for leaving.

I'd covered about a half-mile when, for the first time, I noticed my surroundings. A farmhouse, vacant for several weeks, stood near the road. I often passed it when I drove into town. Now the dense shade of an ancient maple tree by the front porch proved irresistible.

I sank onto the bottom porch step and dropped my head to my arms. *If I'm going to get away by noon, I'd better get packed,* I thought.

Then I heard a faint, questioning "Meow?" and looked down to see a small white cat. Was it the animal I'd seen earlier along the fencerow? Probably. Foraging. By the looks of its emaciated little body, it hadn't had much success. For a moment I forgot my self-pity. "Why, you poor half-starved creature," I exclaimed. "I'll bet they moved out and left you!"

The scrawny kitten leaped on the step and tried to crawl into my lap. Instantly I regretted my words of concern. *I'll have trouble shaking her*, I thought in exasperation. I stood up and hurried out of the yard. But she came tumbling after me crying, circling my feet, trying to rub against my legs.

I stopped. She sat down in front of me, looking up into my face. "Now listen, cat," I said firmly. "We don't need a cat. I don't *want* a cat. So, scram! Get lost!" Her gaze never wavered.

I was about to pick her up and drop her over the fence into a cornfield when a large truck came bearing down on us, traveling much too fast for a country road. It thundered by, and when the dust cleared, the cat was gone, apparently terrified into headlong flight.

I walked back along the road, still brooding about leaving. Before I reached home, an idea came to me. We owned a cabin on a lake about four hours north. No telephone. No mail service. I'd just pack and go there. And I wouldn't leave a note for Andy. At first he'd think I'd gone on an errand. But when I hadn't returned by nightfall, he'd look in the bedroom closet and find my bag missing. He might do some calling around; then he'd probably conclude I'd gone to the cabin. But he wouldn't know for sure. He'd be angry—and he'd be worried. *Well, let him worry*, I thought grimly. *When he's concerned enough, he'll come after me. And he can apologize.*

I had nearly finished packing when that inner voice accosted me again: *What if he doesn't come after you? What if he won't apologize? He has a lot of pride, you know.*

Well, I was proud, too! Still, in spite of the heat, I felt a chill of apprehension. I couldn't recall ever going out, even on an errand, without leaving a note saying when I'd be back. And what if he didn't come after me? Would I come crawling home? Would this resentment remain, like an ugly, unhealing wound, between us? We loved each other deeply. But we had friends our age who'd loved each other too, until an act of rejection, like the one I contemplated, became the first step toward separation—and eventual divorce.

Again I probed for the hurt inside me. It was still there. I felt my cheeks burn with anger, and the apprehension died. I zipped my bag firmly shut and hurried into the hall and out the back door.

My car, thank goodness, was filled with gas. I tossed my bag on the rear seat and backed out of the garage. Then I glanced at the seat beside me. The local newspaper I'd bought the day before lay there. By chance—or maybe it wasn't chance—I'd left it in the car when I'd carried the groceries into the house. Now one of the headlines on the front page caught my eye, "Boy Scouts Sponsor 'Be Kind to Animals' Program." *Be kind to animals.* The words seemed to leap out at me.

Animals? The cat! I'd completely forgotten her! Now the memory of the small helpless creature tugged at me. And for the second time that day I forgot my self-pity. How could I have been so heartless? *"Inasmuch as ye have done it unto one of the least of these . . ."* (Matthew 25:40). Did God mean cats, too? I had no choice. I had to go back. And, remembering how the truck frightened her, I decided to walk.

"She's just a tramp," I told myself. "She'll be long gone by now—and I can leave with a clear conscience."

But she wasn't gone. When I approached the cornfield, she came bounding out, as if she'd been expecting me. And perhaps she had. She followed me home and into the kitchen.

I warmed milk for her and cut up some leftover chicken. "Go ahead, eat," I said, placing the food on the floor. I expected she'd gulp it ravenously like most hungry animals. I was wrong. As I turned to the refrigerator, I heard that same faint, questioning "Meow?" I looked down. She sat at my feet, her little face raised to mine.

"You've got food," I said in exasperation. "No self-respecting cat turns down chicken."

She raised a paw and timidly touched my leg. "Meow?" she cried again.

"What *is* it?" I said, picking her up. She nestled close to me, purring ecstatically, then rubbed her head against my cheek. Finally, she settled contentedly against my neck, singing that ridiculous little song.

So that was what she wanted! Love. Unbelievably, it was more important to that starving cat than food or drink. Love. The basic need of all God's creatures. Including me. *Including Andy*, I thought with a pang.

I placed the cat by her food and stroked her gently while she gobbled the chicken and lapped the milk. And I thought back through the previous afternoon and through the morning. That inner voice, the walk, the newspaper headline, the cat—all working together to keep me from leaving. Was it a conspiracy? Suddenly I knew it was. God's conspiracy. Long ago I'd learned he sometimes uses unusual channels to save us from self-destruction.

I breathed a sigh of thanks. Then I remembered something I'd forgotten. No matter how good a marriage is, there are bound to be times of bitterness, of dissension, of wanting to "get even." The marriage vow is "for better, for worse," and we all need to build reserves of kindness and forgiveness to help us through the bad times. Because, as the little cat had just reminded me, love is by far the most important thing we have.

Stroking the soft fur, I searched once again for the angry resentment inside me. It was gone. The cat had finished eating, so I picked her up. Looking into her eyes, I said, "Andy doesn't like cats." She yawned, showing her pink little tongue. "But I love you," I added, "so he'll love you, too. He's that kind of guy."

SHE LOVED ME MORE THAN SHE HATED MY CATS

MARION BOND WEST

I grew up living next door to a tall, widowed woman with no children. She walked to work at the drugstore and walked home because she didn't own a car. She looked stern with her dark hair pulled back into a perfect ball. She always wore sensible black shoes, long-sleeved dresses, and an antique pin.

"Miss Margaret," as I was taught to address her, hated cats. I adored cats. My cat Josephine was forever having kittens in Miss Margaret's immaculate garage. Miss Margaret would see me out playing and call, "Yoo-hoo, Marion. Come here, please."

I'd run to her out of breath, and often she said without a trace of a smile, "Your cat has had kittens in my garage—again." I would look up at her, nodding, chewing on my lip—and hoping. "They can stay there . . . this time." Miss Margaret and I went through this routine each spring and fall. I'd breathe a sigh of relief and take off for her garage to see the newborn kittens, calling out over my shoulder, "Thank you!"

Back then I didn't understand why Miss Margaret allowed Josephine such a luxury, but I didn't spend a lot of time pondering the matter. Lately, though, when the delicate pink and green spring days that smell of hyacinths and daffodils return, I think of Miss Margaret. I smile now at the clear evidence that Miss Margaret loved me more than she hated my cats. And I'm reminded that love isn't always "fussy." Sometimes it's hidden in a simple yet bountiful statement, "All right, this time."

IN NEED OF LOVE

SCOTT WALKER

*O*ur two cats, Tuxedo and Tiger, have been with us for a long time. Born in the same litter twelve years ago, they have moved with us through three states and have watched as three children have been born into our family. These cats are special members of our clan, though they have always lived outside. Fiercely independent, they roam their territory and fight their battles, but they are always home for supper.

Their appetites appear to have doubled, too. Now they stay around the back and meow for food every time the door is opened. Strangely, they often beg loudest when their bowls are brimming over with their favorite food. At first, such behavior perplexed me. For a while, I thought they might be having a problem with parasites, but our veterinarian assured me that was not the case. Then one day the explanation became perfectly clear to me.

The only time I had ever been able to pet these independent felines was when they were preoccupied eating. But once they left the food bowls, they were impossible to catch. So now, when they want more affection, they feel that they have to beg to be fed in order to be petted.

I guess people are the same way. As a pastor, I hear a lot of folks complain about many things. But behind most of the laments, there is a deep hunger to be loved and appreciated. Wise is the person who can see through the crazy ways people asked to be stroked and then simply give them a pat on the head or a warm embrace. After all, they are not really hungry. Their plates are full. They are simply in need of love.

THE SURPRISE IN THE BOX

MARY LOUISE KITSEN

*T*here's more to do than I can handle," I said loudly and clearly. Of course, there was no one to hear my complaint except the three cats lying on the bed. Two of them continued sleeping while the third laid her ears back and switched her tail.

I sighed. There were writing assignments to be done (I'm a full-time free-lance writer), my cousins were coming from Kansas in a few days, and I felt I had to clean the entire house. And my mother was in the hospital again, which meant two trips there each day. How would I get to everything?

Deciding that Jesus was the only one who was listening, I addressed him directly this time. "With your help, I'll make it, but please, don't let anything else happen right now."

It was still early in the morning. I slipped my robe on and started downstairs. Maybe if I relaxed briefly with the morning paper at the same time, I'd feel ready to tackle the busy day ahead. I opened the door and picked up the newspaper. Then I saw the box.

Where did it come from? It was a large box with "Corn-Flakes" written on the side. An old, rusted window screen lay on top; a rope kept it in place. Oh, no . . . someone who knows how I feel about cats must have dumped some kittens on me again. Just what I needed!

I started to pick the box up, and when I felt how heavy it was, I thought, "They've dumped the mother cat too." Actually, I didn't know the half of it!

I set the box down in the living room, untied the rope, and looked in. There was a big yellow cat. But where were her kittens? I reached in and lifted the cat out. It started to purr immediately and pushed its head tightly against my shoulder. One big cat? A male at that.

I held the cat up to take a better look at him and started to sob. This big beautiful cat had no eyes— just white skin where his eyes should have been. I cradled him as my other cats started to gather. Pip-Squeak rubbed against the newcomer with evident pleasure. But what was I going to do with a blind kitty? How much care would he need?

I looked in the box to see if there was anything else and found the note: "This is Poppy. My dad hates having him around and said he'd shoot him if Mom and I didn't get rid of him ourselves. Please take care of him." It was in the handwriting of a youngster. Poor, sad child trying to keep a blind cat alive.

Poppy ate with the other cats—to my surprise and relief—and I showed him the litter box. I got absolutely nothing done before it was time to leave for the hospital, and I worried about leaving the cat in a strange place. But he seemed content and interested in investigating things. I called the vet's office and made an appointment. Then I left, praying that Poppy would make out all right.

When I returned home, I found Poppy sleeping with Pip-Squeak in the sunny dining room window. In the early afternoon I put him in a carrier and headed for the vet's office. I hated to take him, but I had to have help in this matter. The vet took him into a back room to check him over. I sat straight as a pin, not knowing what to expect.

The vet finally came out. He was alone. My heart did a flip-flop. What about Poppy? At that moment I realized the big yellow cat had stolen my heart.

"Someone took good care of that fellow," the doctor told me. "He's in good shape and amazingly contented. We'll keep him a couple days. He should be altered and have some shots, and there are a few tests we'd like to do."

I grinned.

Then the bomb fell: "We think Poppy is deaf and dumb as well as blind."

For the next two days I wondered how I'd manage a pet that couldn't see, hear, or make a sound. I prayed about the cat. And, to my surprise, I was getting an awful lot of things accomplished even though my mind stayed on Poppy. It was as though Poppy was a challenge and so everything else was a challenge too.

I brought Poppy and my mother home from their respective hospitals just two days later. I went for Mom first and got her settled in her favorite chair in the living room. Then I went for Poppy.

Mom moved to the edge of her chair as I brought the carrier in. I opened it, and Poppy climbed into my arms. How he loved people! I carried him over to Mom, and she gathered him to her. In minutes, Poppy purred happily on her lap. It was the start of a warm, personal friendship between an elderly lady and a special kitty cat—a relationship that has made both of their lives happier.

Poppy had helped me too. I was feeling sorry for myself when he came, but through him I gained a better attitude. It seemed almost as if Jesus had helped guide Poppy's owners to the act of bringing him to me. Little by little I began to think more and more about the mother and child who had left Poppy in my care. Who were they?

Would they wonder about what had happened to Poppy?

And then one day I made a sign that said "Poppy is fine" and taped it to my front porch. I hoped the youngster who had brought the cat to me would see it.

The sign stayed up for several days. Then came the morning I went outside to the garage and saw something that made my life even better. Written on the bottom of the sign I'd made were two messages, evidently written by the child and mother—or that's what I've always thought. The child's writing said, "Thank you." The adult's hand wrote, "God bless you."

BED OF ROSES

MARION BOND WEST

I was overjoyed when my husband, Gene, surprised me with a beautiful Persian area rug.

For years I had admired them and wished that one day I could own one. It was perfect in front of our fireplace, picking up the dark green, beige, and rose colors of our living room. As we stood admiring it, our cat, Minnie, stepped cautiously onto the plush rug and settled down in the center of a bouquet of pale pink roses.

"No!" I raised my voice. Our dear Minnie was surprised because she had unlimited access to every square inch of our house, and now I was trying to train her to respect this one bit of space. That night I got up to find Minnie back on the rug, sleeping on the roses once again. I scolded her, and she left reluctantly. Perhaps I *was* a bit overprotective, but for now, while the rug was brandnew, I didn't want to risk it getting soiled.

Then, very early one morning, I came downstairs and discovered that Minnie had positioned herself so that the tips of her front paws barely touched the fringe of the rug; the rest of her was safely not touching it at all! She looked at me very innocently and pitifully, purring as if to say, "Surely you can't object to this!"

Well, I finally felt a little silly. Minnie just wanted a soft, comfortable spot to nap, and she seemed to enjoy those pink roses. After all, this wasn't a museum, but a living room, a room to live in. How could I turn away anyone, human or animal, seeking safety and warmth?

"It's okay, girl," I assured Minnie. She purred with her eyes closed and her paws barely touching the fringe of the new rug she so loved. I went back to bed happily and drifted off to sleep thinking: *In any contest of wills between humans and felines, I know who usually wins.* Sleep came quickly.

We all seek the comfort of God's sheltering arms. My own "bed of roses" is in the warm safety of his love.

THEODORA, GOD'S GIFT

JoLynne Waltz

Several months ago I moved eight hundred miles away from my family to start my first job after college. I loved my work. But coming home to the emptiness of the apartment I'd rented—that was no fun!

Early one morning I was awakened by what could only be the meowing of a cat—and it was close by. I got up to investigate. In the kitchen, I found the back door open—I was certain I'd locked it the night before—and, to my amazement, there was a tattered, green-eyed tiger cat striding imperiously around the room. Quickly I made a search of the apartment. Nothing was missing; nothing had been tampered with. Reassured, but puzzled, I knelt to pet the cat. She nuzzled against me, purring contentedly.

A few days passed, and no one in the neighborhood claimed her and no one advertised for a lost cat. By that time it would have been hard to give her up—we clearly enjoyed each other's company.

"I guess it's safe to name you, my friend," I told her. I'm going to call you 'Theodora.' "

That night, during my weekly phone call home, I told my mother about my new four-footed roommate.

"I'm glad you have a pet, JoLynne!" she said. "I've been worried about you being so lonely. In fact, I've been praying about it every day." And then she chuckled. "Where ever did you get that name—'Theodora'?"

"I don't know, Mom. It just came to me out of nowhere—the way she did."

What neither of us knew then—but I learned later—was the derivation of the name "Theodora." It's from the Greek: *Theo*, God; *dora*, gift. Theodora—the cat, like her name, God's gift!

LEO THE LIONHEARTED

SUSAN DEVORE WILLIAMS

*F*irst, you should know that this isn't just another cat story. The main character is, I admit, my Siamese cat, Leo. I can't tell you that Leo ever dragged me from a burning building or croaked his deafening Siamese meow to warn me of an impending earthquake. But God has used him to teach me a lesson it's taken me twenty years to learn, and not many cats can be *that* kind of hero.

From the moment our eyes met through the pet shop window one cold spring day, I knew this sealpoint kitten was something special. He struggled and protested loudly as the shopkeeper pulled him from his cage.

"He may be small," I laughed, "but he seems to have the heart of a lion."

"He has the voice of a lion, too," the shopkeeper said. And so I named him Leo the Lionhearted. Even his birthday seemed symbolic. Valentine's Day.

My husband and I were childless and, as often happens, we became more than casually attached to Leo. He managed to fit himself into every area of our lives effortlessly and completely. I grew to expect his noisy greeting at the door each evening, and I enjoyed his flattering, rapt attention when I wandered around our apartment doing housework. He even developed an awareness of my moods, pawing at my leg to be picked up when he sensed I needed comforting, then patting my cheek with his paw.

Sometimes I'd catch myself carrying on an animated conversation with Leo as he'd perch on a chair and gaze at me. "If I could be that kind of listener," I told him, "I'd be the most popular woman in town." And Leo never disagreed with me.

In his third year, Leo stayed with my parents while we were away on an extended business trip. When we picked him up he was listless and very thin. My father had tried everything to coax him to eat, to no avail. His belly seemed bloated, and within a few hours it had grown so large he had trouble sitting down. I called his veterinarian. "Bring him to my office now," he said.

At the clinic, the vet made a quick diagnosis: a kidney stone. "Another hour and he'll be dead unless I take some emergency measures. I don't guarantee anything. He's in a lot of pain. Do you want me to go ahead and catheterize him, or should I put him to sleep?"

I stood in numbed silence. Words wouldn't come. Finally, I shook my head. "Do what you can to save him. Please."

I sat in the waiting room until, at long last, the vet returned. "I don't know what to tell you. I've catheterized him, but he's passed another stone, and I'm afraid this is going to be a chronic problem. He needs surgery, and I doubt he'll survive it. He's very underweight and weak. If it were my cat, I'd put him to sleep."

"Does he have any chance at all for recovery?" I asked.

"I'd say no," the vet said. "I'm sorry, but I know you want the truth. He may have a five or ten percent chance of surviving surgery, but he will always have this problem."

"I need some time alone with him, please," I managed to say.

When the vet left me in the examining room, I stroked Leo's fragile body and watched him breathe. Until that moment I hadn't realized how much I'd come to love my lionhearted cat.

"Lord, I can't kill him unless you tell me to," I said aloud. "You're going to have to give me some sort of confirmation, or else you're going to have to do it yourself. Show me, Lord." I waited.

Perhaps five minutes passed, and I stood stroking Leo's head. He was very still. Suddenly, a thought entered my head: *Pray for him. Pray for his healing.* I laughed bitterly. "Pray for an animal? I'm really cracking up!"

After a few moments, my heart racing, I put both hands on Leo's body. "In the name of Jesus, you are whole. In life or in death, you belong to God. I commit your spirit to God, who created you." I paused. "Father, I ask you for Leo's life. Please restore him to health. Thank you, Lord. I trust you with his life."

The vet walked into the room as if on cue, looking expectantly at me.

"I want you to operate," I told him. "Do whatever you can to get him through the night. I'll talk with you in the morning."

"Okay," he said reluctantly. "But I don't think he'll survive the surgery."

By morning, as I prayed, my faith was about half the size of a mustard seed. I dreaded calling the vet.

"Well, sometimes animals will surprise you," he said. "He made it through the night. But he's a very, very sick cat. I can't give you any real hope. Do you want to see him?"

Leo was an even more pitiful sight than he'd been the night before. I should have let him be put to sleep. But deep within, I could feel God's gentle reproof: *Where is your faith? You asked me for restoration. Trust me!*

I stroked Leo's head, and he slowly raised his eyes to my face.

Oh, Lord, I thought, *he trusts me so completely. Even in this pain, he trusts me. I want to be like that with you. Help me trust you in my pain. Make me like that, Lord!*

I moved my hand under Leo's throat and ever so faintly I felt a vibration. He was purring.

The following morning, the vet called to warn me that Leo was now only four pounds, would not eat at all, and would have to be force-fed if he was to survive even another day. "It might give him an extra will to live if you took him home," he said. "Being in familiar surroundings might help."

Hastily, I prepared for Leo's return: padded box with a heating pad, bottles of baby food, eye droppers for liquids.

"Okay, Lord," I said on the drive to pick him up. "It's up to you."

Through the next twenty-four hours I attempted to feed Leo every fifteen minutes. Because he was unable even to lick water, I squirted it into the side of his mouth. Most of it dribbled out onto the towel I'd wrapped around him. He gazed at me with unblinking eyes. I scraped baby food onto his lower teeth, but it simply lay on his gums. Finally I sat beside Leo unmoving, weariness sapping my strength, and I said, "Lord, should I stop? Show me. I need to know your desire, your intentions."

I put one more fingerful of food to Leo's mouth and started to open his lips. Then I watched his tongue slowly reach out and lick the food from his teeth, and then from my finger. I let out a whoop and jumped to my feet.

I had an impulse to read a psalm of thanksgiving, and I reached for my Bible. Leafing randomly through the psalms, I began to read aloud, not really thinking deeply about the words, until they began to sink in as I reached this verse: "For every beast of the forest is mine, and the cattle upon a thousand hills. I know all the fowls of the mountains: and the wild beasts of the field are mine" (50:10-12).

Stunned, I read the words again and again, feeling the heaviness lift from my heart. "Lord, how wonderful you are," I prayed. "Leo's yours, and he's always in your mind. Thank you for lending him to me, for making him my trusting friend. Thank you for showing me that I need to be that kind of trusting friend to you."

Within forty-eight hours, Leo was walking shakily and eating normally. In a week, he was recovered. In three months, his weight was up to nine pounds.

"Just don't expect this to be permanent," the vet told me when I took Leo for a checkup. "At any moment, he could get another kidney stone, and that'll be it."

Over the next two years I rejoiced in Leo's good health. But I also developed a kind of chronic fear as a result of the vet's dismal prognosis. I watched Leo daily for signs of recurrence. If he sneezed, I called the vet. Finally, toward the middle of his fifth year, it happened: the same symptoms, but I caught them before the bloating got out of hand. In a state of panic, I raced to the vet.

By this time, fear had a good grip on me. "Lord," I said, "is this it? Two short years? I thought you'd healed him completely." I felt a pang of guilt. I wasn't doing a very good job of trusting God, I thought. *No, I could feel the Lord saying deep inside, you aren't.*

It turned out that Leo had a serious infection, and he nearly died again.

Leo recovered, of course. And in his seventh and ninth and twelfth years, he had similar brushes with death. Each time, my confidence in God's intentions grew. But the fear didn't leave entirely. I prayed over and over that God would remove it.

In Leo's sixteenth year, we moved to California. There, my life entered a phase that hardly seemed real. My husband of eighteen years left me. But I got "custody" of Leo. Once again, he spent long hours at my side, comforting me with his presence.

Then, just a few weeks after my husband's departure, Leo developed symptoms of infection. "No, Lord!" I cried. "I can't go through this now! Don't take him away from me! Don't do this!" Fear seemed more powerful than ever. I was so distraught that without pausing to think, I found myself speaking in a loud, angry voice: "Stop it! Just stop."

Who—or what—was I speaking to?

Fear, I thought. *That's what.*

"Stop," I said again, angrier than ever. "Fear, I am sick of you. This cat doesn't belong to me. He belongs to God. The Lord has healed and restored him over and over again, when everyone said it was hopeless. So it's time you just got *lost.*"

Amazed at my own words, I smiled. And then I felt it. The fear *had* departed. I was calm. I gathered up my lionhearted cat and told him, "Don't worry. You're going to be fine. As usual."

But that night, as I lay in bed, the emotional pain of my broken marriage began to overwhelm me. Leo would be all right, I knew, but what about me? I was nearly forty, without any kind of support system in this strange city. I had no future, no career, no money, no home, and my friends and family were more than two thousand miles away. "Lord," I whispered into the night, "what will become of me? I'm so *afraid*."

Leo padded from the foot of the bed toward my face. His cold nose touched my chin. In the darkness, he settled down to comfort me again. "Leo, I'm so scared," I told him. "I'm so *scared*." He purred and licked my cheek. Slowly, the truth began to dawn on me.

God had taught me to trust him for my cat's life. It had taken most of Leo's proverbial nine lives to do it. Each time he'd approached the brink of death and all had seemed hopeless, God had done the impossible. I could almost hear him say, "How many times are you going to have to go through this before you finally learn to trust me?"

Yet God had done the same things in my life that he'd done in Leo's! Events crowded through my mind as incident after incident played out like a movie. Time and again the Lord had met my need—and in ways I'd never expected. Had he ever abandoned me? Had he ever failed to provide food, clothing, shelter, work, friends, and everything else I needed? Had he ever broken his promises?

I hugged Leo close. "We're going to be okay," I whispered.

And we were.

Leo's had skirmishes with death in the last four years, but the fear has not returned. His new vet pronounces him one of the Seven Wonders of the World.

"He's probably your oldest friend," the vet said on her last visit to check Leo. "It's going to be terribly difficult for you when he finally goes."

I thought about that. Yes, it will be hard. It can't be anything else. But the fear—well, we've gotten through that together, Leo and I. And we've learned about trusting God, together. The Bible told me that Leo is God's and, in a loving and miraculous way, God has revealed himself to me through the lionhearted cat.

I scratched Leo's ears and smiled. The vet stroked him admiringly.

"I'll say this for him," she said. "He's sure lived up to his name."

Editor's note: Leo lived to the ripe cat age of twenty-one. He died of old age just three days after his birthday.